*An Album of*

# SOUTHERN

# BIRDS

AMERICAN EGRET

# An Album of
# SOUTHERN
# BIRDS

Photographs by

## SAMUEL A. GRIMES

Text by

## ALEXANDER SPRUNT, JR.

1953 · UNIVERSITY OF TEXAS PRESS · AUSTIN

*To* Ann
*for patience, understanding, and*
*encouragement*

# List of Plates

*with photographic data*

8

# Samuel Andrew Grimes

*A Biographical Introduction*

# Samuel Andrew Grimes

"No sooner had my head cleared the rim than a bomb seemed to burst in my face. The wire-mesh helmet which came down to my heavily padded shoulders was driven violently back against my nose from which blood immediately streamed. I all but lost my precarious hold upon the edge but, clinging there long enough to collect my senses, I started to back away, fighting the demons off as best I could."

This is not the description of a front-line incident in Korea or the experience of a Marine on a Japanese held island, but just another, if somewhat unusual, adventure of Samuel Andrew Grimes in bird photography. It happened during his attempt to secure pictures of the home life of the Great Horned Owl on a pitch black night in a cypress swamp near his home in Jacksonville, Florida.

Sam Grimes had been visiting the nest of this owl for some years and had banded the young on several occasions. In order to make a photographic record of the food brought in by the old birds, he had planned to rig the camera at the nest with a linen thread running from it to a blind on the ground. The latter was so placed as to allow him to see the silhouette of the bird as it alighted on the nest, even on a dark night. Because of former visits he thought the owls had become accustomed to him; indeed, he says, "they were friendly in a reserved sort of way and only hooted at me from a respectable distance." So, one evening he set out with all his gear ready to spend the night at the nest site. While there was still light enough to focus the camera, he started up the tree.

"The first thing I knew," he relates, "I was slugged two blows across the shoulders in rapid succession from opposite directions. The owls had literally crossed me up. One would alight in a tree on one side, the other on the opposite. I nearly wrung my neck off trying to keep an eye on both at the same time so that I could duck, but it wouldn't work. They struck again and again and nearly ruined my woolen jacket. That I could stand and, so far, had only a few nicks on the shoulder; but when I got to the nest and stuck my head over the edge, one owl slammed me full in the face and ripped open my lower lip, which proceeded to bleed profusely. The front of my jacket and shirt were quickly soaked with blood. With the unpleasant thought that the owl could just as easily have hooked me in the eye, I pulled the remains of the jacket over my head and made as precipitous a retreat as possible, soundly beaten. The scar on my lip has faded some but my recollection of the incident has not.

"Do you think I had sense enough to let those owls alone? No. Instead, I devised a sort of owl 'mask,' consisting of a fibre helmet with a 'veil' of quarter-inch hardware cloth that hung from the rim of the helmet to my shoulders. No frenzied owl was going to drag its talons through my eye or jugular. It was with no little satisfaction that I set forth a few evenings after my debacle to show the owls that they had met their match. I had my shoulders well padded and even wore gloves, but the mask was my ace-in-the-hole.

"The owls had calmed down not at all; they belted me right and left, working the old crossfire routine to perfection. They struck the helmet a few times but did no harm. I went on up and set up the camera; dark came and I got in the blind. Hours passed but the birds would not come back. They just hung around in the vicinity and hooted. At 2 a.m. one did fly to the nest and even though it had brought nothing in, I felt I had better shoot the picture, and did.

"This meant that the film and flash lamp must be changed. I set out, mask and everything in place, in the pitch dark, to climb the tree, whereupon the owls lit into me with such fury as they had never shown before. As I think back on it, I must have been a determined sort of cuss for I went on up despite the hammer blows."

Then came the violent climax at the nest rim which is described in the opening paragraph of this sketch. Sam Grimes called it quits. "I finally got the camera down and never put it up again," he said.

The vicissitudes of the nature photographer only rarely involve real personal danger; more often they consist of petty annoyances and frustrations; sometimes they are ludicrous in the extreme. Take the case of the Gray Kingbirds, for example.

Having located a nest of Gray Kingbirds in the top of a mangrove, about 15 feet high, Grimes set about rigging his equipment, which entailed some considerable trouble. Finding some very muddy, oyster-encrusted two-by-fours in the vicinity, he constructed a sort of tower on top of which he fastened the camera focussed on the nest. A black thread ran from it to the blind which was some 150 feet away amid the foliage. Gray Kingbirds are notoriously averse to photographic equipment staring them in the face, and this pair proved no exception to the rule.

After roosting in his blind on a camp stool for an hour or two, Grimes felt the tide rising about his feet. Later, it was up to his knees and still the uncooperative birds did nothing. When the water reached his chest he gave up and climbed into the mangroves, lugging the blind with him, and re-ensconced himself among the limbs.

Three hours crept by and at last one of the birds began to approach the nest. Realizing that it was just a matter of time now, Grimes sat tight. Then something happened. A female Red-winged Blackbird spied the black thread in mid-air and decided it was just what she needed for her nest lining. She alighted on a convenient twig and proceeded to tug at the line vigorously. The watcher in the blind broke his silence violently, but the only result was that the Gray Kingbirds were effectually frightened away again.

14

The blackbird continued to yank at the thread and actually set off the sensitive solenoid-operated shutter. Another climb to the nest was thus necessary and the whole procedure started over again from scratch. Again the Redwing returned and tried earnestly but this time Grimes had tied the thread around a branch in such a way as to require a pull stronger than the bird could manage. After a siege of some seven to eight hours, he finally succeeded in getting what he called "one very ordinary picture."

Sam Grimes was born at Carlyle, Kentucky, May 5, 1906, but has lived most of his life in Florida. His interest in birds began at the age of five (Cardinals and Blue Jays were the species first to attract him), and it grew until it pervaded his entire life. However, it always has been and still is a hobby, which is why my thoughts of Sam Grimes are constantly tinged with regret—regret that he did not make his hobby his profession.

I do not mean to imply that his photographs would have been better if he had become a professional ornithologist, but there would have been many more of them, and his contributions to man's knowledge of birds would have been much more extensive. His name in ornithology, as prominent as it is, would have been even more so. Therefore, as an ornithologist, I wish that Sam Grimes had devoted his life to that science. Certainly, however, his profession—that of an engraver—has contributed to his hobby, so we will forgive him.

As it is, Sam Grimes' amateur status is high on the ladder. In 1925 he became an Associate of the American Ornithologists' Union. Elevation to the class of Member in this organization came to him in 1951, which meant national recognition of his contributions to ornithology. This honor was all the more unusual because he had been able to attend only one meeting of the A.O.U. prior to 1951 and, by his own admission, did not possess an extensive bibliography, "not much written stuff." He is also an enthusiastic and valued member of the Wilson Ornithological Club and the Florida Audubon Society.

Let's look at him again in the field, where he really is at home. I watched him once when we were together on the Kissimmee Prairie in Florida as he dumped his equipment at the base of a cabbage palm (palmetto) in the crown of which was the nest of a Caracara. He wanted a photograph of it. There was no lost time in this undertaking, no indecision, figuring on this or that angle, or measuring of distances. He rigged the camera as though he could have done it blindfolded, strapped on climbing irons, looped camera over shoulder and stamped up the smooth trunk of the palm as easily as one walks upstairs. A wide leather belt looped about his waist and the tree left him free to manipulate the cumbersome Graflex, and in an amazingly short period the job was done.

Sam Grimes and birds' nests are practically synonymous. His ability to find them borders on the uncanny. Even in a country utterly new to him, he ferrets them out as surely as a good pointer on quail. Disclaiming any formula for it, he simply shrugs it off characteristically and says that there is "nothing to it." That there *is* something to it is evident to anyone who has ever been afield with him. "I lucked up a nest" is a typical Grimes description of one of his finds. His "luck" is amazingly consistent.

Although a great amount of his field work and photography has been in Florida, Sam Grimes has worked in many other states. Even though he may be unfamiliar with the region, the nest-finding technique always works. I recall vividly that he stopped in Kerrville, Texas, in the summer of 1950, when I was attached to the staff of the Audubon Camp there. One of the great avian attractions of that locality is the Golden-cheeked Warbler which occurs only in a very limited area. I had had classes in the field to see the bird consistently for three summers but we had never found a nest. I had also looked about during off hours with no success. Sam was a visitor there for two days and found a nest of the Golden-cheek on his first try. "Lucked it up," no doubt.

Having attained the degree of proficiency in nest finding which he has—and that is as near perfection as any mere human can reach—there is no wonder that his work has appeared in publications far and wide. Anyone familiar with bird photography anywhere must be equally familiar with the words beneath many of the finest of such pictures: "Photograph by S. A. Grimes." A complete list of these publications would indeed be impressive, but I could get nothing more out of the photographer than "most American periodicals and some foreign."

Knowing as much about bird behavior and home life as he does, he would be the first to admit that he still has much to learn. But he has at times been in a position to gather knowledge that even his "superior" scientific confreres may be ignorant of. For instance, bird books have long stressed the extreme secretiveness of the rail family, which may be said to reach its ultimate in the nesting habits of the Black Rail. A thorough reader of the literature, Sam Grimes gathered that photographing a Black Rail on the nest would be an almost superhuman achievement. Nevertheless, and possibly because it offered such a challenge, he determined to try it. Here is what he says of the experience:

"When I finally had an opportunity to match my wiles against the little birds I felt that my somewhat extensive experience gave me a definite advantage. I would focus my camera on the nest, run a remote control line back a good distance, go away for a time, then sneak back to the end of the line and pull it to spring the shutter.

"I spent the better part of a hot July morning sneaking up and pulling that thread at about half-hour intervals. I wanted to be sure that I'd have at least one good pose. I could not of course see the nest from the end of the thread. The next day when I developed the plates I found that I had drawn all blanks. I recall how impressed I was with what I considered the wariness of the Black Rail.

"Some time later I was fortunate enough to be shown another nest of this elusive bird. I was determined to try again, and this time I would run the line so far back that my approach could not possibly be detected by the sitting bird. I proceeded to trim and bend aside the obstructing vegetation, and as I reached near the nest, something darted up like a streak and pecked me on the finger. I instinctively jerked my hand back, and there, with feathers all

16

ruffed up, stood the diminutive Black Rail in her tiny nest of eggs. She protested and threatened as I finished my preparations and photographed her at will.

"I know now that I could have sat at the first Rail's nest and secured all the pictures I cared to take. The approach to the remote control line had undoubtedly in each instance caused the bird to run from the nest, which would be her natural tendency. I sure figured that one wrong."

He had figured it wrong because he did not know any better than to believe what had been written about the bird for years.

Another observation which certainly upsets the usual idea of a bird's behavior took place only a few weeks ago when he was working with the Black-whiskered Vireos in the Tampa Bay area. Now vireos have never been described in the literature as particularly pugnacious or aggressive. They are woodland birds, entirely insectivorous, deliberate in movement and rather dull and inconspicuous of plumage. The Black-whisker is a tropical cousin of the Red-eyed Vireo which Roger Peterson calls the commonest bird in the United States. As far as I know it has never been photographed before. Little is known of its way of life other than that it supposedly parallels that of its well-known relative. Here is what Sam Grimes found out about it during his vigil at the nest.

"While I sat quietly in a rowboat near the nest there occurred something that I would never have believed. The birds were going about their business, feeding the young ones and singing (which either sex does equally well) when there appeared near their nest another Black-whiskered Vireo. Just who attacked whom it was impossible to tell but there was an explosion of commotion followed by a fight of such violence as I have known only in game-cocks. The two birds tangled in a death-grip that was released only after they had fallen, wildly splashing, in the water; and no sooner had they fluttered back again to the mangrove twigs than they lit into each other again. Four times they tumbled into the water before one bedraggled bird made off through the trees. And I thought vireos were dignified, peace-loving birds!"

Thus does the watcher in the blind add to ornithological knowledge. Unseen and unheard, he is afforded opportunities which the unconcealed observer is denied. To some, hours of waiting for a bird to return to the nest may be nothing more than a necessary evil; to others they open a new world.

It seems to me that few occurrences of importance in ornithological history are so marked by well merited justice as a recent discovery which crowns Sam Grimes' nest-finding career. During this century there have been a fortunate few who have found the first nest of such-and-such a species in such-and-such a state. Even the first in a region, even the continent (Blue Goose and Bristle-thighed Curlew are examples). All were, however, birds native to North America.

On May 5, 1953, Sam Grimes discovered the first nest in North America of an exotic species which had entered the United States not through man's introduction, but of its own volition, the first time this has taken place in recorded history. The bird is the Cattle Egret (*Bubulcus ibis*).

An African species, it was introduced into British Guiana some years ago under circumstances not yet entirely clear. In March of 1952 it appeared in some numbers in the Lake Okeechobee region of Florida and subsequently has been seen along the Atlantic seaboard as far north as Massachusetts. Its advent caused excited speculation regarding its future spread, possible nesting, etc.

Believing that it had already nested in Florida, Grimes determined to look for it in the most likely locality and, with Audubon Warden Glenn T. Chandler, he succeeded in presenting himself with a most memorable present on his forty-seventh birthday. Sloshing through hip-deep water, beating down cattails with one hand, shoving aside mats of water hyacinths with the other, he and Chandler fought their way into a maze of willows and buttonwoods, where hundreds of herons and ibis circled and squawked about their rude stick homes.

Sizing up the rookery to determine a likely vantage point from which observations might be made, the two men erected a small platform a few inches above the water and set the blind upon it. Then Chandler left Grimes in the blind and made his way back to their boat.

Four hours passed in the steaming tropical heat. Then suddenly there appeared two Cattle Egrets. Grimes' heart pounded with excitement as the beautiful birds tiptoed their way down through a tangle of willows to a scanty nest of twigs only 15 feet or so from his hiding place. The egrets stayed on the nest for about twenty minutes, billing and strutting, rearranging the twigs, and otherwise engaging in courtship activities. The nest held a lone egg, the very first of its kind to be found on the continent.

The following month Grimes found and photographed the first nestling Cattle Egrets, adding these epochal pictures to those of the nest and egg and attendant adults secured earlier. There is not one of his friends, acquaintances or admirers but will rejoice that he is the one to whom this history-making honor has come. Certainly, no one better deserved it than the prince of nest-finders.

It is, of course, inevitable that Sam Grimes has been asked, time and again, how he secures his pictures and what his technique is. He replies that he has "no particular technique." And he goes on to add that "conditions differ tremendously in bird photography and it is largely a matter of adapting the equipment to fit the job at hand. Oftener than not, the bird photographer is compelled to do a good bit of improvising."

Improvisation sometimes has its complications. On one occasion Grimes journeyed to one of his favorite hunting grounds, Merritt's Island off Florida's east coast, to secure some Barn Owl pictures. This is what took place.

"I set up the equipment in the attic of a badly dilapidated house. It was a dark night. I set the camera up at dusk, focussing by flashlight, hung the blind from a rafter, settled myself and waited. My plan was to work by ear. I would hear the bird alight in one of the many openings to the attic; she would shuffle her way to the eggs, and when all had quieted down I would set off the flash.

"An hour or two passed. It got very dark. All that was visible to the eye were the holes in the roof through which could be seen the starlit sky. I heard some hounds barking in the distance. (This shack was in an isolated location, and I suppose coon and 'cat' hunting was good in the vicinity.) The dogs were working my way—I could tell by their barking becoming louder—and then I could even hear the hunters' voices.

"In a short time the dogs were scarcely a hundred yards away, and I commenced to get uncomfortable lest the dogs 'tree' me in the old attic. I stuck it out till they were practically breathing down my neck, but when one of the gun toters cut loose at my sanctuary with a couple of rounds of birdshot, which bounced off the wooden shingles and rattled among the rafters, that was too much.

"I slipped out of the blind and switched on the flashlight in order to sweep up my camera and other paraphernalia for a hasty departure. As I did I turned the light on to the owl nest just in time to see a five-foot rat snake slither away with two owl eggs in his belly and another in his mouth. Bird photography is great fun."

And of course, there have been experiences without complications, canine, ballistic, or otherwise. Some of them have concerned owls, too. Let's look at one.

A pair of Screech Owls were nesting in a fence-post cavity and offered a chance of a picture showing arrival at the hole with prey. Setting up his equipment as late as daylight would allow, Grimes entered the blind and settled to his vigil. In the pitch darkness he had to depend on his ears again, so, only 5 feet from the post, he listened intently. He knew well enough that he could not get any sound from the owls' wings but he thought he could hear their claws on the wood when they alighted.

All was black and still for some time. Then at last "there was a definite thump and recognizable scratching of talons on dry wood." He pressed the cable release and a blinding flash followed. And says Grimes, "When I say blinding I mean exactly that. My iris diaphragms had become so widely dilated in the almost total darkness that they were at their greatest natural aperture, and the volume of light admitted by the flash was quite blinding. I saw not a thing. But I did have hopes the bird was there."

"A day or two later I developed the film, and when I lifted the negative out of the hypo I experienced one of the greatest thrills that has ever come to me in my photographic work. The picture I had secured far exceeded my fondest expectations. Not only did I have the bird that had just alighted on the post but his mate, with her face filling the nest entrance."

And this thrill can be shared by many, for that picture is in this volume and speaks eloquently for itself.

Another question often asked Sam Grimes is, "What camera do you use?" Again let him answer in his own words:

"I reply that I have several. Then some ask which I consider the best for bird photography. To which I am constrained to answer that that depends upon the conditions under which a bird is to be photographed. The BeeBee type camera is best for this, the Leica best for that, and so on. I know of no camera that has all the features that are best for all sorts of bird photography. I could very well get by with my Graflex, Leica, and folding camera, but I usually have six or seven along. It is not lack of equipment but lack of time that has restricted my hobby."

This very lack of time has always been one of the reasons why I have regretted that Sam Grimes is a professional engraver instead of an ornithologist. In the years from 1936–1941 when I was Supervisor of Southern Sanctuaries for the National Audubon Society, I was obliged to make monthly inspection trips to Florida to check on wardens, equipment, and wildlife. Time and again I practically begged Sam to go along. Sometimes he did, more often he did not. He wanted to, yes, but . . . . Now and then, he would meet me at some designated place by leaving work in the late afternoon and driving all night, arriving in the morning ready for a day's photography. Having accomplished it, he would get back in the car, drive back to Jacksonville, and be at work in the morning. No man can stand a great deal of that. Sam carries no excess weight, but still it has been a marvel to me for years to consider how he does what he does. What *could* he accomplish if it were not for his everlasting engraving business? You see my point?

The advent of artificial light in connection with field photography was, of course, a great boon. Probably many operators now wonder how they ever got along without it. As might be supposed, Sam Grimes seized upon it at once.

"I took up with flash lamps the moment they were put on the market and even made my own synchronizer. I had tried flash powder before there were lamps but with little success. The flash lamp has its shortcomings but does make possible the photographing of birds under conditions of poor lighting that would otherwise be extremely difficult. The strobe light does the same thing but is less reliable and more awkward to use. For the strictly scientific purpose of showing feather arrangement and other details of the aerodynamics of flight the strobe light is invaluable, but in my opinion a more appealing picture of a bird in motion can be made in daylight or in a combination of daylight and photoflash lamp, and there can be no question about such a picture having a more natural appearance than a strobe shot.

"I have had strobe lights since the time they became reasonably portable. In every instance where I have used the strobe I have obtained better pictures of the same subject with other light. Take the hummingbird for example; the strobe light arrests the wing motion completely, and what do you have? A bird that looks as if it were suspended by invisible wires. I prefer the picture in which the bird looks alive (see the picture in this volume). What sort of a picture would it be without that full sweep of the tiny wings? I have the 'arrested' kind too, but this is what I like. It was shot at only 1/200 second, and took me a lot longer and a bit more film than if I had shot at 1/5000, because flight pictures are hard to get right at slow exposures."

From the earliest days of nature photography the strategy of tricking wild things into taking their own pictures has been followed with varying degrees of success. Grimes says that he has used it frequently because it is a timesaver. While some photographers use elaborate photoelectric equipment that operates like a "magic door," Sam conceals a simple electric contact device where the bird will alight or walk. It works equally well on the ground or in trees. The pictures in this volume of the Broad-winged Hawk and the King Rail are examples of it. The operator can set such a device, then go off on other investigations and return later, the film having been exposed in the interim.

In recent years, again because of the time saving element, Grimes has relied more and more on the Leica and long-focus lenses. He can work from a greater distance; in most cases the farther any unnatural objects are placed from the nest, the more readily will a bird return to it. The pictures of the Cattle Egret and Pine-woods Sparrow in this book are Leica shots. All of them are from Kodachromes. Another advantage of the Leica is that color film in the 35 mm. size is not nearly so expensive as in the cut-film sizes. This is an important consideration when operating a motor-driven camera by remote control from a distance too great to see or hear the movement of the mechanism. He says that he has often taken eight or ten exposures where one or two would have sufficed, but that he was glad to get one good shot out of a lot.

"The Everglade Kite picture (in this book) is one of a series made with the Leicamotor," Grimes says. "The water was waist deep at this nest, and the nest was five or six feet above it, so we fastened a bamboo extension to each leg of the the tripod in order to get elevation. Then we ran a line 100 yards and waited in the boat. The male bird went back to the nest in about two hours' time. The female came no nearer than to circle overhead. It was the male that flushed from the eggs and that showed great concern at our intrusion. At another nest some miles away, which held newly hatched young, it was the male that was brooding and that returned to the nest. The female hunted snails, and on a couple of occasions I saw her bring the extracted animal to the vicinity of the nest, whereupon the male flew out to meet her, took the snail from her beak as they hovered in flight, and brought it to the young. This has nothing to do with photography, but it does point out what a bird photographer notices."

Let's qualify that a bit and say what *some* bird photographers notice. It is this very combination of photographic technique and ornithological knowledge which has made Sam Grimes' work the tremendously valuable contribution that it is.

Another of the methods long used is that of the dummy camera, set up and left for the birds to become used to. Grimes says that he has used it when he has had time to "follow up." Though a timesaver in the long run it is of no use when one is in a hurry. However, Grimes is of the opinion that there are times "when no picture would be had at all if a dummy were not used to 'break the birds in.'" A case in point is the photograph of the sitting Great Horned Owl in this book. Sam set up the dummy a week before he took the picture. The dummy was a box with a hole in it on a platform in a tree about fifteen feet from the nest. When he

21

was ready for business, Sam placed a Graflex under the box, ran a line a hundred yards off to a gallberry patch and "in a matter of minutes I had the picture."

Now, you may well ask, "What about color pictures?" In this day when color photography is rapidly gaining the ascendancy, the question is certainly pertinent. Once more, let's see what Grimes has to say about it.

"When a color film practical for use in bird photography became available, I jumped on it with both feet and after a few experiments found that by wrapping my flash bulbs in blue cellophane I could get good synchro-sunlight shots. The flash was necessary because of the slow speed and high contrast characteristics of the emulsion which made a 'fill-in' light indispensable. Blue flash lamps appeared on the market a long time afterward. The Red-bellied Woodpecker picture in this book is from one of the old Dufaycolor films, which came on the market before Kodachrome.

"A short time later 35 mm. Kodachrome was announced, and I adapted a 6⅜″ lens to a Bantam camera in order to use the film with a lens of desirable focal length. In this I met with reasonable success also, and made many color shots with this rig. Unfortunately the dyes in this early Kodachrome were unstable, and the color films that I have left from this period are all badly faded.

"Then Ektachrome took the place of professional Kodachrome and I immediately gave it a whirl. Some of the results have been rather pleasing. The Canada Warbler (this volume) is Ektachrome; the Cardinal is Kodachrome professional, and the Everglade Kite and American Egret are miniature Kodachromes."

Sam Grimes was a pioneer in the use of color in ornithological photography. One of his color shots, that of a Roseate Spoonbill, was reproduced in the issue of *Bird-Lore* (now *Audubon Magazine*), the official organ of the National Audubon Society, for September–October, 1937; it was possibly the first full-color photograph of a wild bird to appear in print in this country. The development of color photography and the reproduction thereof has been so rapid that it is difficult to realize that less than twenty years ago it was a rarity.

These then, are glimpses into the life of a bird photographer. It is not, as we have seen, all sweetness and light, but the fascination of it and the way it has added to the ever growing popularity of bird study must be evident.

I feel sure that, even though my attempt to introduce you to my friend through the medium of words may be inadequate, all who view his magnificent photographs in this volume will join me in saluting an able field ornithologist, excellent technician, fascinating raconteur, and amiable gentleman, Samuel Andrew Grimes.

ALEXANDER SPRUNT, JR.

Charleston, South Carolina
July 15, 1953

22

*An Album of*

# SOUTHERN

# BIRDS

BROWN PELICAN. This dignified throwback to antiquity
seems more like a contemporary of the dinosaur or the
pterodactyl than a twentieth–century bird. Superb
diver, strong of wing, master of uniform flight.

25

WATER TURKEY. Remnant of the Age of Reptiles, the Snakebird is almost a modern icthyornis. A strange, silent dweller in cypress gloom and willow swamp—remote, fantastic, unearthly.

GREAT WHITE HERON. Looming hugely in multi-colored waters, an animated iceberg in a tropic sea. Largest of the herons, its normal range is restricted to Florida Bay, Cape Sable and the Keys.

MARSH BIRDS. Birds against the grass, a colorful tapestry at rest, kaleidoscopic patterns in the air. Living movement amid living green; crowning touch to any inanimate scene, however beautiful.

REDDISH EGRET. A nonwhite egret? Yes. At home amid the mangrove flats of the Florida Keys, the low, huisache-cactus islands of Texas. Once sought by avaricious plume-hunters, now by eager bird-watchers.

Snowy Egret. Frequents cypress swamps and marshes from New Jersey south to the Gulf Coast. Once reduced to practical extinction because of the plumes worn by both sexes, it is again abundant through protection.

29

CATTLE EGRET. Africa, South America, now the United States! First exotic species to appear of its own volition —a history-maker of modern ornithology. A yellow-billed "Snowy," companion of cows and magnet of field students.

First found nesting in North America by Samuel A. Grimes, the Cattle Egret is today one of the most talked of birds of the continent. Its further spread is very probable—watch for it!

30

WOOD IBIS. Actually no ibis at all, but the only American stork. Uncouth and clumsy at rest; magnificent aloft in soaring grace.

AMERICAN BITTERN. A bird, or a patch of brownish cattail? Stiff, still, or swaying with the reeds; over-looked, passed by, but—there it is! An animated, silent, but eloquent example of protective coloration.

GLOSSY IBIS. Found with consistency only in the vicinity of Lake Okeechobee in Florida, the Eastern Glossy's apparently white face is a narrow band of light skin, not feathers as in the western species.

WHITE-FACED GLOSSY IBIS. Decurved beak, beautiful re-
flections from bronzy plumage, white about the face—
what could this be but an ibis, glossy, white-faced?

33

WHITE IBISES. For years the "food bird" of southern swamps and marshes. A rookery nester *par excellence*, in flashing red and pure white, touched with jet. Accomplished aerialist, graceful feeder, companion of egrets and herons.

Roseate Spoonbill. Unbelievably pink, peculiar, and prehistoric! Dweller of the Florida Keys and Texas coast, once much persecuted by the feather trade, now rigidly protected and increasing.

There is no more beautiful sight than that of a flock of Roseate Spoonbills emerging from the mangrove shadows to wade in the multi-colored waters of Florida Bay.

35

RING-NECKED DUCKS. Jaunty cruiser of cypress lagoon and marshy pool; black, white, and gray with banded beak; now up, now down. Close cousin of the Scaups but an individual of parts, a wildfowl aristocrat. The other ducks in the picture are Lesser Scaups.

BLACK VULTURE. Darkly somber, silent, funereal. Corollary of death, decay and dissolution, yet serving the living by consuming that which taints and poisons—these are the vultures.

TURKEY VULTURE. On fence-post or road shoulder, a bareheaded, clumsy, and repulsive scavenger. Aloft, the epitome of soaring grace, a feathered master of aerodynamics.

TURKEY VULTURE NESTLINGS. Incipient garbage collectors which, if disturbed, become garbage dispensers. Even a short distance lends enchantment to little buzzards.

38

EVERGLADE KITE NESTLINGS. So like the Marsh Hawk,
and so different. Dangerously low in numbers today,
restricted to a tiny range in Lake Okeechobee, Florida,
this bird's future is precarious, for its food consists of
a single kind of freshwater snail.

RED-SHOULDERED HAWK. Natural control on rats and mice in field and woodland, the Red-shoulder is too often misunderstood and persecuted through ignorance of its food habits because it takes an occasional chicken.

EVERGLADE KITE

BROAD-WINGED HAWK. Another easily seen "soaring" hawk, the Broad-wing is blamed for the acts of its hard-to-see relatives, Cooper's and Sharp-shinned Hawks, or Darters. A rodent eater and an aid to agriculture.

BALD EAGLET. A regal, imperious infant, destined to swing aloft magnificently in kingly flight. Now nest–bound but far from helpless even in natal down.

OSPREY. Spectacular cruiser of the air; impressive diver
from the heights; builder of bulky homes in cypress la-
goons, mangrove thickets, or towering pines, the Osprey
is the fishing hawk supreme.

AUDUBON'S CARACARA. Eagle, hawk, or vulture? Actually this unusual bird is all three! At home on Florida prairies, Texas lowlands, and Arizona deserts. Stately in walk, strong in flight, hunter of living prey but not disdaining carrion—the Caracara.

BLACK RAIL. What was that slipping through the grass— a mouse, or a swiftly moving shadow? No, a bird, tiny, silent and mysterious, known only to those who seek diligently in marsh and oatfield.

KING RAIL. Master of concealment; elusive ghost of
grass, cattail and marsh; now here, now there. Living
basis for the expression "thin as a rail."

WILSON'S PLOVER. Dweller by the sea, at home amid dunes, shells, and sand. It leads intruders away from speckled eggs or downy young by "broken" wing tactics. Its clear, whistled notes blend with wind and surf.

BLACK-NECKED STILT. Pipestem legs, as bright as they
are, prevent the Stilt from attaining complete grace. But
delicate bill, black and white plumage, and "spectacled"
head make it an unforgettable bird.

RING-BILLED GULLS. Wheeling, circling, weaving—gray and white forms of grace and airy lightness, tracing bold patterns against the sky—these are the gulls.

RING-BILLED GULLS. Birds of the air and water, equally
at home in both. Harbor scavengers, ocean wanderers,
sometimes inland nesters—the distinctive Ring-bill.

COMMON TERN. Long narrow wings, forked tail, pearl gray mantle over snowy underparts, and a black cap—these are the terns, or "sea swallows." Once persecuted for their plumage, now rigidly protected and increasing.

WILLET. Plain gray and white at rest, spectacular in the air, with black and white flashes in the wings. Noisy, active denizens of beach and marsh, filling the air with their clamorous "pill-will-willet."

BLACK SKIMMER. Amazing beaks; colonial nesting;
clumsiness at rest, and delicate grace aloft—these add
up to the Black Skimmer, that "sea-dog" of coastal fish-
ermen, whose yelping cry is often heard at night.

MOURNING DOVE SQUABS. Squat, ugly, and fat—little promise now of the trim, streamlined grace to come. All but overflowing their flimsy home, these young doves are the Cinderellas of the bird world.

GROUND DOVE. A tiny avian knight in scaled armor; a
dainty walker among domestic poultry; gentle, confid-
ing, and attractive. Never molested in a country where
"dove" means only a gamebird to many.

53

YELLOW-BILLED CUCKOO. "Oh, Cuckoo, shall I call thee bird or but a wandering voice?" Shy, elusive haunter of the shades; "rain crow" of the country boy; trim, stream-lined nemesis of bug and caterpillar.

BLACKED-BILLED CUCKOO. Slovenly and frail as their homes may seem, American cuckoos keep house themselves, unlike their parasitic European cousins. The uniformly dark bill and minimum amount of white in the tail set this species apart.

BARN OWLETS. Queer, peering caricatures— young Barn Owls, ever hungry for a mouse. The Barn Owl's breeding habits are peculiar; fresh eggs are frequently found in the nest with almost fully grown young.

BARN OWL. Half monkey, half bird? No. Just a capable rodent control, a bird which helps crops to grow and feed a mighty nation. Should we encourage its continued existence? You answer that one!

SCREECH OWL. Natural camouflage *par excellence!* Find the erect gray phantom in its gray retreat. Owl and Spanish moss are perfectly blended.

An eerie, tremulous whistle in the night bespeaks the presence of this small, fluffy gray or red destroyer of mice and insects, who is far more often heard than seen. Whistle Owl really, rather than Screech.

SCREECH OWLS. Two of a kind, returning from a nocturnal foray, meet at their fence-post home. A remarkable picture, secured in pitch darkness by the photographer who heard their claws on the wood as they alighted.

SCREECH OWLETS. Three of a kind out on a limb, two toes forward in the best owl fashion, match stare for glare with the camera lens.

GREAT HORNED OWLET. A youngster fierce and indomitable even in infancy, worthy offspring of parents living by rapine.

GREAT HORNED OWL. Powerful, rapacious, and impla-
cable—such is this great bird. Good or bad? Neither—
simply filling a niche in nature's economy far superior to
our ability to sit in judgment.

BURROWING OWLS. Long-legged "hornless" clowns of Florida's prairies, golf courses, and dairy pastures. They nest underground in a dead-end tunnel as much as seven feet long which they dig themselves. Their flight is a series of bounding undulations usually ending with a comical bobbing curtsy when the bird alights.

BARRED OWL. Villified, persecuted, misunderstood; mouse-eater, rat-catcher, and general aid to the farmer, helping him produce our food! Why not stop cutting off our noses?

CHUCK-WILL'S-WIDOW. A clear, insistent chant among the live oaks; a wandering voice at night. A fitful waft of wing; a dark shape lengthwise on a limb; a cave-like mouth; a flying insect trap—mysterious, unseen but . . . "chuck-will's-widow."

CARDINAL

Nighthawk. A mouth with wings! An aerial harpist, streamlined and graceful. At home on city roof-top or remote sandy flat, wavering against the sunset, calling "peenck-peenck."

RUBY-THROATED HUMMINGBIRD. Infinitesimal, but mighty in spirit; a flashing gem in glowing feathers; epitome of perfect flight and throbbing life—the Ruby-throat.

66

YELLOW-SHAFTED FLICKER. A woodpecker on the ground? Yes, because this one is an ant-eater. Over five thousand ants have been found in a single stomach of a Flicker, which perhaps you know as Yellowhammer.

PILEATED WOODPECKER. A regal patrolman of the forests, crested in scarlet. Destroyer of wood-borers, grubs, beetles, and worms. Almost crow size, the largest of the woodpeckers except the vanishing Ivory-bill.

RED-COCKADED WOODPECKER. A touch of red, a black and white shape on a pine trunk, digging, boring into the bark, destroying that which destroys the tree.

HAIRY WOODPECKER. An oversized Downy with large bill and without black bars on the outer tail feathers. Less common than its smaller relative.

RED-BELLIED WOODPECKER. "Zebra-back" would be a better name perhaps, though there is a red wash on the lower abdomen. Noisy inhabitant of town or woodland.

DOWNY WOODPECKER. Small edition of the Hairy Woodpecker. The Downy is a favorite with feed-tray enthusiasts over the country, for it has a wide range.

CRESTED FLYCATCHER. A large, crested, yellow-bellied flycatcher, at home in town or country. Nests in cavities or bird-boxes in which cast snakeskin is invariably used. Often known as "freight bird" in the South. (*above*)

COUCH'S KINGBIRD. A yellow-bellied, olive-backed, notch-tailed Southwesterner. From Arizona to the lower Rio Grande it occurs locally and uncommonly, its way of life similar to that of the other kingbirds. (*below*)

PHOEBE. Easily recognized by its "phee-bee" call. Nests under bridges, porches and rock ledges. Uses exposed perch from which it sallies forth after insect prey. Sits erect like all flycatchers.

70

ACADIAN FLYCATCHERS. The elusive "wicky-up" notes, echoing through dark cypresses and willow brake, come from this plain, almost drab little swamp dweller. The frail nest seems no more than scanty strands of moss.

71

WOOD PEEWEE. Few birds "say" their names as clearly as this one. Slow and plaintive, reminiscent of drowsy summer days in the pinelands, the dreamy notes sound softly from afar.

ROUGH-WINGED SWALLOW. A small, dark swallow not widely known. Nests in loose colonies, burrowing into banks and bluffs like miniature kingfishers. Different from the Bank Swallow in that it lacks a breast band.

Barn Swallow. The only member of the family with a "swallow tail" (forked). Rapid, graceful flier, nesting in barns, under bridges, and at times in caves. Day migrant, feeding as it goes on its vast migrations.

PURPLE MARTIN. "Straight as a martin to its gourd"—
Indians thus attracted the bird originally, plantation
slaves continued the practice, we follow suit. No struc-
ture is more acceptable, no matter how elaborate.

SCRUB JAYS. So Floridian as never to be recorded outside
that state (except as other races). No crest, no black and
white. Often a yard bird, it is easily induced to eat from
one's hand. Jaunty, noisy, attractive.

TUFTED TITMOUSE. The only small, gray, crested bird. Nests in bird-boxes and natural cavities. Its clear, whistled "peto-peto-peto" is a familiar sound in Southern swamps and woodlands as well as yards and gardens.

Perhaps this is an unfair advantage to take—a cut-away peek at the domestic affairs of the Tufted Titmouse.

CAROLINA CHICKADEES. These sprightly black, gray, and white birds are distinguished by their tiny size, their pleasing whistle, and the intense activity in which they are nearly always engaged.

Brown-headed Nuthatch. A tiny resident of the pine-lands, neighbor of Red-cockaded Woodpeckers and Pinewoods Sparrows. It digs its own nesting hole. Chattering flocks cruise high from tree to tree.

WHITE-BREASTED NUTHATCHES. Upside down, right side up, crosswise; gray and white acrobats in feathers; searchers of cracks and crannies, destroyers of bugs, beetles, and borers.

LONG-BILLED MARSH WREN. A bubbling trill from the marsh stems, a tiny brown shape creeping into a globular grassy home swaying in the reeds. Noonday sun or midnight darkness are all the same to "Tom-tits."

80

MOCKINGBIRD. The best known avian Southerner. Match-
less in song; proficient in mimicry; alert, streamlined,
and attractive, needing no brilliant feathers to enhance
its wide popularity.

81

CATBIRD. Somber of plumage but a pleasing vocal performer, this dark dweller of thicket and tangled brush is a favorite with many. The mewing call note gives rise to its common name.

82

CURVE-BILLED THRASHER. Spines and thorns hold no terrors for this bird, which well knows the value of *chevaux-de-frise*. Desert sands, rocky arroyos, and cholla-dotted flats are home to the Curve-bill.

Wood Thrushes. Best known of the thrushes, filling woods and gardens with liquid melody. Welcomed in spring, enjoyed all summer, their departure in fall for the tropics is always regretted.

A big mouthful for a big mouth. Thrushes, like human parents, know how hard it is to fill the "bottomless pit" of a juvenile stomach.

BLUE-GRAY GNATCATCHERS. Trim, tiny, and alert, miniature mockingbirds in appearance. Their high, insect-like
"zee-e-e" note and beautiful lichen-adorned nest are
characteristic of their dainty attractiveness.

RED-EYED VIREO. According to Roger Tory Peterson, the commonest bird in the United States. Deliberate searcher among shade and forest trees, its slow, oft-repeated song is delivered through much of every summer day.

MIGRANT SHRIKE. The "French Mockingbird," all dressed up. Stocky build, black line through eye, hooked beak, and sharply contrasting blacks, grays, and whites denote the Shrikes. Their practice of impaling insects and mice on barbed wire and thorns give them the name of "butcher-bird."

MOUNTAIN VIREOS. These vireos look as if they were
wearing spectacles. Mountain nesters in the South, they
invade the lowlands in winter. Often found in moss-
hung oaks unhurriedly searching out insect prey.

BLACK-WHISKERED VIREOS. Southerners indeed, living on Florida Bay, Cape Sable, and the Florida Gulf Coast. The fluffed feathers of the male obscure the mustache line. Rarely if ever successfully photographed before.

CANADA WARBLER

SWAINSON'S WARBLERS. Elusive phantoms of swampy
lowlands, their ringing song drifts eerily over blue
palmetto, cane, and cypress, ever luring one on into the
shadowy fastnesses.

PROTHONOTARY WARBLERS. The very spirit of the cypress country—gray and golden birds whose clear, whistled melody peals bell-like from leaning stub, mossy log, or the entrance to their nesting cavity.

MYRTLE WARBLER. From Northern spruce forests this warbler invades the South in winter to forage in multitudes among the myrtle thickets and pinelands. Its sharp metallic "chip" and yellow rump distinguish it.

PINE WARBLERS. Well named indeed. At home in long-leaf and loblolly pines, searching the tufts of needles, sometimes clinging to the trunks like nuthatches. The simple trilling song blends with the chitter of the Brown-headed Nuthatch and the chirr of the Red-cockaded Woodpecker.

BLACKBURNIAN WARBLER. A blaze of black and orange
against the dark shades of Blue Ridge spruce and bal-
sam, the Blackburnian voyages each fall into the tropics
where its brilliance seems really more at home.

93

PRAIRIE WARBLERS. Olive-green, brilliant yellow, and jet black, a color combination which commands attention in the Florida mangroves, the Gulf Coast scrub, the Carolina brushlands, and northward.

OVENBIRD. Much like a miniature thrush, but really a ground warbler with heavily striped underparts and a golden-buff crown patch. The nest on the ground is like a "Dutch oven." The loud, ascending song is usually rendered as "teacher, teacher, teacher."

LOUISIANA WATER-THRUSH. Although actually warblers, Louisiana Water-thrushes are more like tiny woodland sandpipers. They not only walk but tip up and down like little clowns. Their songs are loud and ringing, with an appealing quality of wild freedom.

KENTUCKY WARBLER. One of many unfortunately named birds. No more common in Kentucky than elsewhere in its range. More often heard than seen, it has a wide black band from each eye down the yellow throat.

96

HOODED WARBLER. A beautiful olive-green, black-hooded, yellow-breasted swamp warbler whose ringing song echoes sweetly down cypress aisles. Usually found at low elevations, like a jewel in its leafy setting.

REDSTART. The "butterfly" of birds, the *candelita* (little torch) of the tropics. Brilliant in plumage, active in habit, flashing its orange wing and tail patches in constant, fan-like display.

BULLOCK'S ORIOLE. Intense orange, black, and white make a startling pattern which this oriole flashes through much of the West and Southwest. The black crown and orange cheeks separate it from others of the family.

FIELD SPARROW. An unobtrusive little inhabitant of the grasslands, whose pink bill will always distinguish it. Its clear trilling song is uttered through the warmest days of drowsy summer.

SEASIDE SPARROW. As characteristic of the salt marshes as the periwinkles which inch up the grass stems from the rising tide. Dingy, frayed looking little birds, but active singers of strange buzzing songs.

PINEWOODS SPARROW. One of the finest songsters of the
sparrow family—a shy, retiring resident of open pine-
lands where it plays hide-and-seek with intruders.

WHITE-THROATED SPARROW. A general favorite in the South in winter, where it utters its plaintively sweet, easily imitated song on mild days. It seems a miniature chicken scratching among the leaves and shrubbery.

CAROLINA JUNCO. A Southern mountaineer, at home atop
the highest peaks of the Blue Ridge and the Smokies,
where its white outer tail feathers flash sharply through
rhododendron "hells" and laurel thickets.

*This book was composed in twelve point Linotype Caledonia, four points leaded. The captions are ten point Caledonia, two points leaded. The display type is ATF Bernhard Modern Bold. The paper is Warren's Cumberland Dull, 100-pound basis, and the binding material is Bancroft Natural Finish Buckram. The monochrome engravings were made by the Respess-Grimes Engraving Company, Jacksonville, Fla., while the color plates were furnished by Thames and Hudson, Ltd., London. The book was printed and bound at The Lakeside Press, R. R. Donnelley & Sons Company, Chicago, Illinois and Crawfordsville, Indiana.*